9/18

THE NIGHT SKY

Giles Sparrow

Published in 2018 by Enslow Publishing, LLC.
101 W. 23rd Street, Suite 240, New York, NY 10011

Library of Congress Cataloging-in-Publication Data

Names: Sparrow, Giles, 1970- author.
Title: The night sky / by Giles Sparrow.
Description: New York, NY : Enslow Publishing, 2018. | Series: Space explorers | Audience: K to Grade 3. | Includes bibliographical references and index.
Identifiers: LCCN 2017031803| ISBN 9780766092662 (library bound) | ISBN 9780766094086 (pbk.) | ISBN 9780766094116 (6 pack)
Subjects: LCSH: Astronomy—Juvenile literature. | Astronomy—Observations—Juvenile literature.
Classification: LCC QB46 .S6958 2018 | DDC 520—dc23
LC record available at https://lccn.loc.gov/2017031803

Printed in the United States of America

To Our Readers: We have done our best to make sure all websites in this book were active and appropriate when we went to press. However, the author and the publisher have no control over and assume no liability for the material available on those websites or on any websites they may link to. Any comments or suggestions can be sent by e-mail to customerservice@enslow.com.

Picture Credits:
Key: b-bottom, t-top, c-center, l-left, r-right ESO: 18bl (Y Beletsky); Getty Images: 9br (Design Pics Inc), 12-13 & 26bl (Babak Tafreshi), 14tr (Oxford Science Archive/Print Collector), 20cl (DEA/G Dagli Orti), 21br & 27cl & 30b (Detlev van Ravenswaay); NASA: 7c (Robert Simmon/Chris Elvidge/NOAA/ National Geophysical Data Center), 17tr; Shutterstock: cover & title page main (SKY2015), tl (TBStocker), bl (Sunti), c (Giovanni Benintende), tr (Pikul Noorod), br (Rigoni Barbara), 4-5 (Stefano Garau), 4cl (MaraQu), 4b (Viktar Malyshchyts), 4cr (NASA), 5t (tose), 5br (pixbox77), 6-7 (Yuriy Mazur), 6b & 26tr (vchal), 8-9 (Yiucheung), 8b (Evgenii Bobrov), 9t (Redsapphire), 10br (Designua), 12cr (Primoz Cigler), 13r (lhovik), 14-15 (SKY2015), 14bl & 26 br & 30t (Vadim Sadovski/NASA), 16-17 & 27tl (Oscity), 16l (I Pilon), 16br (HelenField), 18-19 &27tr & 31b (Petri jauhiainen), 18c (Wantanee Chantasilp), 19r & 30tr (Muskoka Stock Photos), 20-21 (MarcelClemens), 20br (Designua), 22l (Marzolino), 23 & 27br (shooarts), 23 b/g (Stephanie Frey), 24-25 b/g (Maria Starovoytova), 24l (Marzolino), 25 & 27bl (shooarts), 26tl (solarseven), 26cr (Vadim Sadovski), 28cl, (MarcelClemens), 28br (Juergen Faelchle), 29cr (Stas Moroz), 29bl indiey; Wikimedia Commons: 17cr (Vokrug Sveta).

Enslow Publishing
101 W. 23rd Street
Suite 240
New York, NY 10011
USA
enslow.com

CONTENTS

Introduction.. 4

Astronomy.. 6

Night and Day... 8

Earth's Orbit 10

Eclipses... 12

Shooting Stars 14

Meteorite Impacts 16

Lights in the Sky...................................... 18

Comets.. 20

The Northern Night Sky 22

The Southern Night Sky 24

Did You Know?.. 26

Your Questions Answered 28

Glossary..30

Further Information 31

Index...32

Introduction

Our Universe is a huge area of space made up of everything we can see in every direction. It contains a great number of different objects—from tiny specks of cosmic dust to mighty galaxy superclusters. The most interesting of these are planets, stars and nebulae, galaxies, and clusters of galaxies.

Stars

A star is a dense (tightly packed) ball of gas that shines through chemical reactions in its core (middle). Our Sun is a star. Stars range from red dwarfs, much smaller and fainter than the Sun, to supergiants a hundred times larger and a million times brighter.

Planets

A planet is a large ball of rock or gas that orbits (travels around) a star. In our solar system there are eight "major" planets, several dwarf planets, and countless smaller objects. These range from asteroids and comets down to tiny specks of dust.

Nebulae

The space between the stars is filled with mostly unseen clouds of gas and dust called nebulae. Where they collapse (fall in) and grow dense enough to form new stars, they light up from within.

Galaxies

A galaxy is a huge cloud of stars, gas, and dust, including nebulae, held together by a force called gravity. There are many different types of galaxy. This is because their shape, the nature of their stars, and the amount of gas and dust within them can vary.

This is our home galaxy, the Milky Way, seen from Earth. Our view of the Universe depends on what we can see using the best technologies that we have.

Galaxy Clusters

Gravity makes galaxies bunch together to form clusters that are millions of light-years wide. These clusters join together at the edges to form even bigger superclusters—the largest structures in the Universe.

Astronomy

Seeing the wonders of space for yourself could not be easier. On a clear, dark night, anyone can stargaze. Special tools such as binoculars or telescopes can help you, but you can also see a lot with nothing more than your eyes.

Ready to Stargaze

To see as much as possible in the night sky, allow your eyes to get used to the dark. If you can, get out into the countryside, away from the glow of nearby cities. Be away from streetlights and phone screens, and do not shine flashlights. After about ten minutes you will find your eyes are much better at seeing faint stars.

Binoculars

If you want to explore more of the night sky, see if you can borrow a pair of binoculars. They are a lot easier to use than a telescope, and you will see thousands more stars than with the naked eye because they pick up more light. They also make everything you view appear larger, so you can see objects such as the Moon in more detail.

Binoculars are an ideal way to get a deeper look at the night sky.

How far can you see without a telescope? All the way to the Andromeda Galaxy, some 2.5 million light-years from Earth!

Many areas of the world are lit up at night. This makes it harder and harder to find really dark skies.

GALAXY PROFILE

Name: Andromeda galaxy
Catalogue number: Messier 31
Constellation: Andromeda
Distance from Earth: 2.5 million light-years
Description: This large spiral galaxy appears as a fuzzy blob of light in dark skies. Binoculars show its oval shape.

Night and Day

Why is the sky dark at night and light in the daytime?
It is all to do with how planet Earth is spinning in space.
Half of the world faces toward the Sun at any one time,
experiencing daytime, while the other half faces away
and has night.

Daytime Skies

Why can't we see stars if we block out our view of the Sun? This is
because Earth's atmosphere picks up and "scatters" sunlight from all parts
of the sky. It glows a bright blue that drowns out even the brightest stars.

Look east (opposite the sunset) on a clear evening and see if you can spot the dark band of Earth's shadow rising up.

Time Zones

People have always used the
movement of the Sun to keep time,
but this means that "local time" is
different wherever you are on Earth.
Faster travel and communication
in the 1800s led to the use of time
zones. Each zone agrees on a standard
time, rather than just using the Sun's
position in the sky.

Greenwich Meridian (time is measured from here)

International Date Line (it is midnight here when it is noon on the Greenwich Meridian)

Full Moon

New Moon

Moon orbits Earth

During the 27.3 days that it takes the Moon to circle the Earth, we see different amounts of its sunlit face. This cycle is known as the phases of the Moon.

Close to Earth's north and south poles, the Sun never sets around midsummer—instead, it just dips close to the horizon around midnight before rising again.

Earth's Orbit

As Earth orbits the Sun once a year, it goes through a cycle of seasons. This is because the planet is tilted, so the northern and southern hemispheres (halves of Earth) get different amounts of sunlight at different times of year.

Tilted Earth

Earth's axis (imaginary line that runs through the planet from pole to pole) is tipped at an angle of 23.5 degrees from upright, and points toward the pole star, Polaris. When the Sun also lies in this direction, it is summer in the northern hemisphere, with a high Sun and longer days, while the southern hemisphere has winter. Six months later, it is winter in the north and summer in the south.

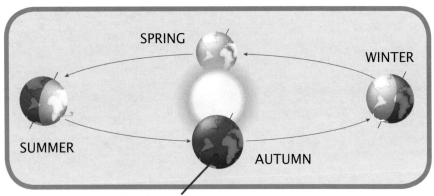

This diagram shows the cycle of seasons in the northern hemisphere.

Wandering Seasons

Although Earth's axis points toward Polaris at the moment, that isn't always the case. The direction of Earth's tilt slowly wobbles in a 25,800 year cycle called precession, and the cycle of seasons wanders with it. Scientists think this cycle makes a difference to Earth's climate, especially during ice ages when the planet is colder than usual.

In spring, Earth's axis points neither toward nor away from the Sun. Day and night are about the same length but the days are getting longer.

In summer, one hemisphere tilts toward the Sun. The Sun rises earlier, sets later, and crosses higher in the sky, warming the ground.

In autumn, Earth's axis once again points neither toward nor away from the Sun. Days become shorter and nights get longer.

In winter, one hemisphere tips away from the Sun. It rises later, sets earlier, and has a less warming effect because it crosses lower in the sky.

Eclipses

Eclipses are some of the most amazing events in nature. They happen when the Earth, Moon, and Sun line up so that the Moon either passes into Earth's shadow (a lunar eclipse) or passes in front of the Sun (a solar eclipse).

Eclipse Effects

During a lunar eclipse, it is rare for the Moon to disappear completely. More often, it turns a coppery or bloody red as it reflects light that has passed through Earth's atmosphere. Solar eclipses are far more impressive, but they should only ever be watched through special safety glasses.

Conditions in Earth's atmosphere affect the look of an eclipsed Moon.

The last rays of sunlight create an effect called the diamond ring.

Eclipse Myths

Eclipses are rare events, and people around the world have often come up with mythical stories to explain them. The Vikings believed that the Sun was being eaten by wolves, while the ancient Chinese blamed a dragon. Even when most people realized that the Moon was creating the eclipse, many still believed that eclipses could bring bad luck.

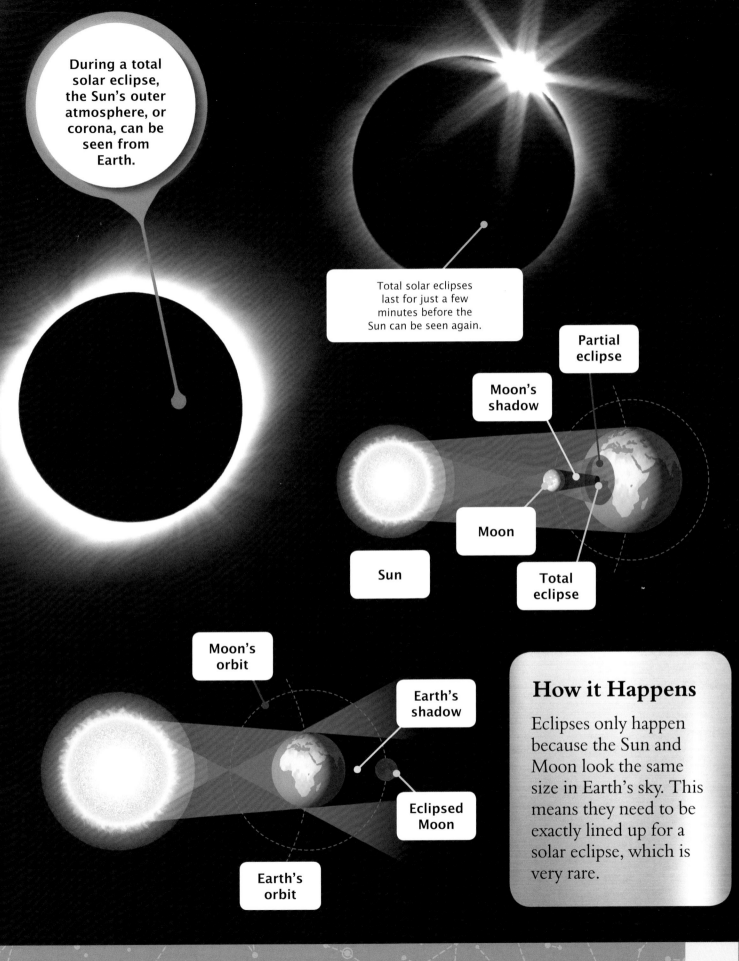

During a total solar eclipse, the Sun's outer atmosphere, or corona, can be seen from Earth.

Total solar eclipses last for just a few minutes before the Sun can be seen again.

Partial eclipse

Moon's shadow

Sun

Moon

Total eclipse

Moon's orbit

Earth's shadow

Eclipsed Moon

Earth's orbit

How it Happens

Eclipses only happen because the Sun and Moon look the same size in Earth's sky. This means they need to be exactly lined up for a solar eclipse, which is very rare.

Shooting Stars

Looking into the sky on any dark night, you may see a sudden flash of light—the trail of a shooting star or meteor. This comes from tiny particles of dust burning up as they enter Earth's atmosphere.

Meteor Showers

The space between the planets is full of dust, so shooting stars happen every night. But there are some intense bursts of meteors that happen at the same time each year. These meteor showers happen when Earth crosses a trail of dust particles left behind by a comet.

This drawing shows the Leonid meteor storm of November 1870.

A fireball that exploded over Russia in 2013 shone brighter than the Sun.

Fireballs

A bright meteor that outshines any star is called a fireball. These objects are sometimes too big to burn up in the atmosphere and actually hit the ground. Others end their descent (fall) with a sudden explosion. Bright fireballs can move surprisingly slowly, and are sometimes mistaken for UFOs.

The Leonids are a regular meteor shower that is strongest in a storm that happens about every 30 years.

When Earth crosses a very dense cloud of comet debris, thousands of shooting stars can fall in a meteor storm.

During a meteor storm, shooting stars can fall like rain.

Meteor Calendar

Name	Date	Direction (constellation)
Quadrantids	Early January	Böotes
Lyrids	Mid-April	Lyra
Eta Aquarids	Early May	Aquarius
Arietids	Early June	Aries
Delta Aquarids	July-August	Aquarius
Perseids	Early August	Perseus
Orionids	Mid-October	Orion
Leonids	Mid-November	Leo
Geminids	Mid-December	Gemini

Meteorite Impacts

Space rocks that make it all the way to Earth's surface are called meteorites, and they can cause a lot of damage when they hit the ground. Large meteorites smash craters into Earth's surface, scatter debris across a wide area, and can even change the weather.

Fragments (small pieces) of meteorite found around the Meteor Crater site show that the incoming space rock was rich in iron.

The Moon records impacts (crashes) from up to four billion years ago.

Meteorite Hunting

Scientists find meteorites interesting because they are often made of material that has not changed since the early days of the solar system. But unless you see it fall, how do you tell a meteorite from a normal Earth rock? The trick is to look for them where no natural rocks should be—in deserts, or on top of the ice in polar regions.

Scientists in Antarctica collect a meteorite lying on top of the ice.

Damage from a 1908 fireball explosion over Siberia

Dangers from Space

The largest meteorites can cause damage far beyond where they land. They fling fiery debris very far and throw huge amounts of dust into the air, blocking out sunlight. Sixty-five million years ago a huge asteroid impact in Mexico helped to wipe out the dinosaurs.

Meteor Crater in Arizona is about 3,900 ft (1,200 m) wide. It was created when a 165-ft (50-m) meteorite landed about 50,000 years ago.

Lights in the Sky

Earth's atmosphere creates many beautiful light effects that can be seen by day or night. They include rainbow-like haloes around the Sun and Moon and even glowing clouds. The most lovely of all are the northern and southern lights.

Particles from Space

The northern and southern lights (aurorae) are created when particles from the solar wind are pulled into the atmosphere above Earth's poles by our planet's magnetic field. As they hit the air up to 90 miles (150 km) high in the sky, they pass on energy, which means they glow in hues from green to red to blue.

Green glows are created more than 60 miles (100 km) above Earth's surface. These are the most common form of aurora.

A halo forms around the Sun when ice crystals in the atmosphere are bending light (just as water drops create a rainbow).

The Zodiacal Light

One of the most beautiful sky effects is also the most difficult to see. The zodiacal light is a glow caused when dust in the solar system is reflecting sunlight. It stretches through the constellations of the zodiac where the planets are usually seen, but it is very faint and can only be spotted in the darkest, clearest skies.

Aurorae trace the lines of Earth's magnetic field, where solar wind particles are arriving from space.

Northern and southern lights can often be seen in polar regions. They sometimes show in areas a little closer to the equator, too.

Ice crystals in the air create a halo around the Moon.

Icy Glows

In cold weather, ice in Earth's atmosphere can bend light in many different directions, creating haloes around the Sun or Moon, and bright "sundogs" in clouds to the left or right of the Sun. A rarer sight are so-called noctilucent clouds—clouds of ice high in the sky that glow because they catch the sunlight long after the Sun itself has set.

Comets

Clouds of icy debris orbit the Sun at the edge of the solar system. Normally these objects are invisible, but when a large chunk of ice comes close to the Sun and begins to heat up, the results can be beautiful. The frozen object becomes the heat-filled core, or nucleus, of a spectacular comet.

Comet Appearances

As a comet nucleus warms up, ice starts to melt and escape as jets of gas. These form a glowing atmosphere around it, called the coma. As the comet gets closer to the Sun, radiation (escaping energy) and the solar wind pull at the coma, creating a glowing tail that always points away from the Sun.

Bright comets can show both a blue gas tail and a yellowish dust tail. The coma, or head of the comet, can easily grow to be larger than Jupiter.

As a comet crosses Jupiter's orbit, it can be pulled onto a much shorter track, orbiting the Sun a lot quicker.

Comets have been seen as signs of bad luck since ancient times. Here, the Aztec king Moctezuma II watches a comet that was believed to show his empire would soon fall.

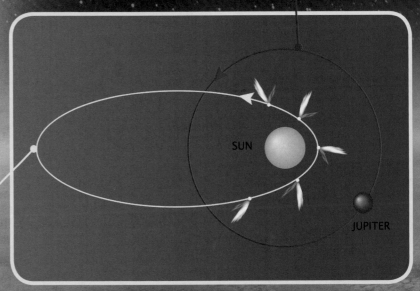

Most comets follow long orbits that only visit the inner solar system every few thousand years.

SUN

JUPITER

Comet Hale–Bopp
of 1997 was the
brightest comet
of recent times.

Comet Tempel 1 shortly
after the "impactor" had
hit its surface.

Exploring Comets

Comets hold deep-frozen material
from the early solar system. This
is one reason why they have
been visited by space probes.
Launched in 2004, *Rosetta* began
to orbit comet 67P in August
2014 and placed a lander on its
surface that November. *Deep
Impact* was launched in January
2005. In July it fired a heavy
"impactor" into the surface of
comet Tempel 1 so that it could
measure the chemistry of the material
that sprayed out.

The Northern Night Sky

In the course of a night, Earth's rotation makes the northern night sky slowly spin around the central pole star, Polaris.

Astronomers split Earth's sky into two hemispheres, or halves, but most people on Earth can see more than half of the sky in a year. People living north of the equator can see all of the northern sky and, depending on where they are, a good amount of the southern sky.

From Earth's north pole, all of the northern sky can be seen.

Northern Stars

The northern sky surrounds Polaris, the pole star that lies directly above Earth's own north pole. Its most famous constellations include Ursa Major (the Great Bear), Leo (the Lion), and Taurus (the Bull). The Milky Way (see page 5) is most visible in the constellation of Cygnus (the Swan), and Virgo (the Maiden) is home to a dense cluster of galaxies.

This old star map shows many of Ptolemy's constellations.

Ancient Constellations

Astronomers split the sky into 88 constellations—areas of the sky marked by a pattern of stars. Forty-eight of these (including most of the northern ones) date back almost 2,000 years to the work of Greek-Egyptian astronomer Ptolemy. His constellations include the even more ancient star patterns of the zodiac, as well as figures from Greek myths such as King Cepheus, Queen Cassiopeia, the hero Perseus, the princess Andromeda, and the winged horse Pegasus.

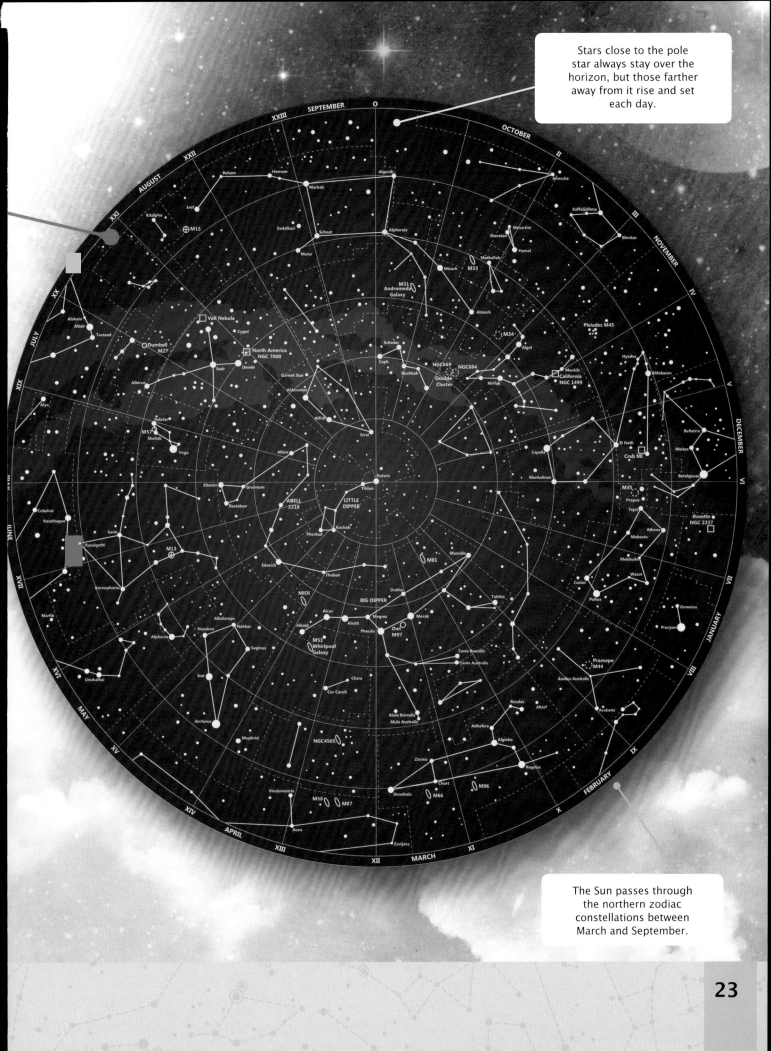

Stars close to the pole star always stay over the horizon, but those farther away from it rise and set each day.

The Sun passes through the northern zodiac constellations between March and September.

The Southern Night Sky

People living south of the equator can see all of the southern sky and, depending on where they are, a good amount of the northern sky. Confusingly, these northern constellations look like they are "upside down" compared to how they are often drawn.

The famous constellation Orion sits on the boundary between northern and southern skies.

Southern Stars

The southern hemisphere is home to the densest parts of the Milky Way, around the constellations of Sagittarius (the Archer), Centaurus (the Centaur), Carina (the Ship's Keel), and Crux (the Southern Cross). Other famous southern constellations include Scorpius (the Scorpion) and Cetus (the Sea Monster).

This map includes the "southern birds," but was drawn before Lacaille added his constellations.

Later Discoveries

Some southern constellations come from the lists of the Greek-Egyptian astronomer Ptolemy, but most of them are a lot newer. One group, named after birds, was described in the late 1500s by Dutch sailors—the first Europeans to see them. Others were filled in later by French astronomer Nicolas-Louis de Lacaille, who worked in South Africa in the mid-1700s. Most of Lacaille's constellations are named after scientific tools.

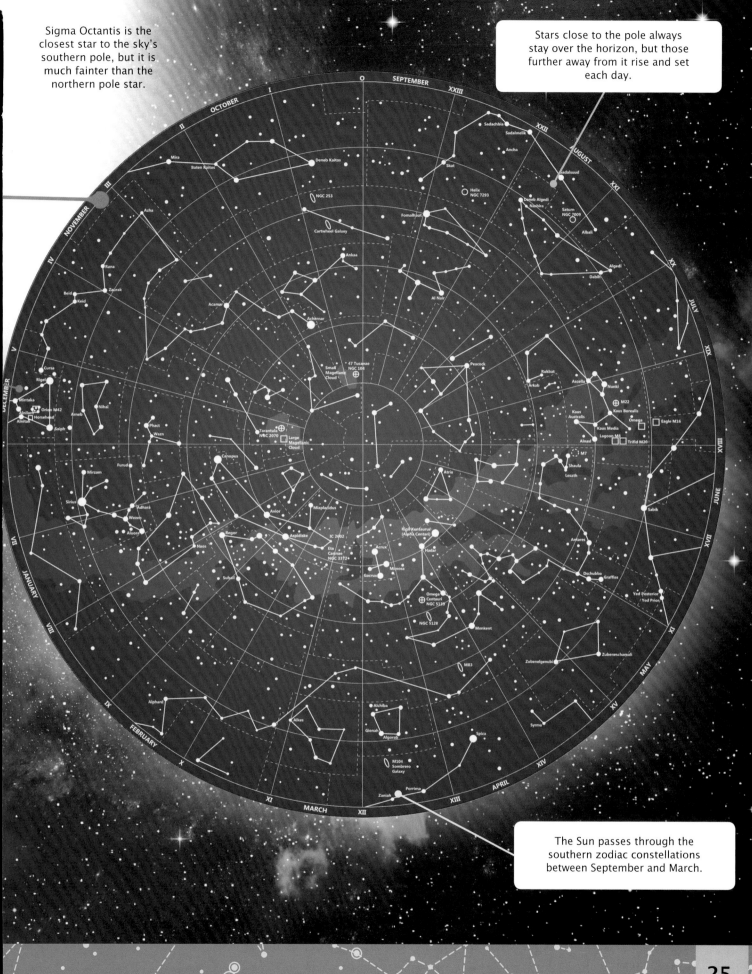

Sigma Octantis is the closest star to the sky's southern pole, but it is much fainter than the northern pole star.

Stars close to the pole always stay over the horizon, but those further away from it rise and set each day.

The Sun passes through the southern zodiac constellations between September and March.

Did You Know?

There's always more to learn about what lies in the vastness of space. Boost your knowledge with these amazing facts about the night sky.

If you need to use a flashlight while stargazing, cover it with red film—your eyes are less sensitive to **red light** so you won't ruin your night vision.

Because the atmosphere scatters the blue part of sunlight away from the Sun itself, the Sun appears to be **yellower** than it actually is.

Mars, Saturn, and Neptune all have very similar tilts to Earth, so they each go through a similar **cycle** of seasons (though over much longer orbits).

Around 200 BCE, Greek scientist Hipparchus used a solar eclipse to work out the **distance** of the Moon from Earth. He got it right to within ten percent!

Bright shooting stars can appear red, yellow, white, or even green depending on the **elements** contained in their dust.

Much of the world's **nickel** is mined at the site of a large comet impact crater in Ontario, Canada.

Rare auroral **storms** can disturb Earth's magnetic field, damaging satellites in orbit and even causing power cuts on the ground!

Sightings of comet Halley, which returns to the inner solar system about every 76 years, have been **traced** as far back as 240 BCE.

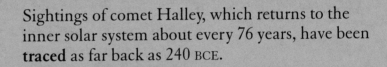

The farther north you live, the **higher** Polaris sits in your sky.

The easiest way to find the pole of the southern sky is to look down the **long arm** of the Southern Cross.

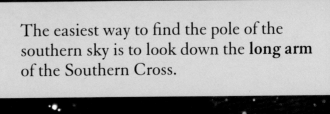

Your Questions Answered

Scientists now know an incredible amount about the night sky, but space is still bursting with amazing information. There are always more questions to be answered and this is what makes people want to become scientists and astronauts. Here are the answers to some interesting questions about space, then you can start asking more!

Do all planets have day and night times?

Yes, all the planets rotate on a central axis and so have times when one side faces the Sun, and the other side is in darkness. One day is the full amount of time it takes for a planet to make one complete rotation. However, each planet take a different amount of time to complete its rotation. One day on Earth lasts 24 hours, one day on Saturn only lasts 11 hours, but one day on Venus lasts 5,832 hours!

How often do eclipses happen?

Lunar eclipses can happen up to three times a year. For the lunar eclipse to happen, the Moon must pass into the Earth's shadow, which blocks sunlight from reaching it.

A solar eclipse happens when the Moon passes between the Sun and the Earth, casting a shadow on the Earth. There are partial or total eclipses, depending on how directly the Moon, Sun, and Earth line up. You have to be in the right spot on the Earth to see it. A total eclipse happens somewhere on Earth around every 18 months.

What if a meteor or asteroid hits the Earth?

Most meteors burn up in Earth's atmosphere and never reach its surface. However, every 2,000 years or so, a meteor big enough to get through the atmosphere without burning up entirely reaches Earth's surface. There is a program within NASA that watches out for objects that pass close to Earth.

Is there a best time of year to see aurorae?

The best time to see the Aurora Borealis is in the northern winter, from September to April. But you also have to consider location. You need to head toward the Arctic and locations such as northern Canada, Alaska, Iceland, or northern Scandinavia. The Aurora Australis is best seen in the southern winter, from April to September.

Do star signs affect your personality?

Some people believe that the movements of planets and stars influence human life on Earth. The study of this is called Astrology. For example, many believe that the constellation prominent in the sky at the time of your birth will affect your personality. It is an ancient science but its claims are very hard to prove.

Glossary

asteroid A small rocky object made up of material left over from the birth of the solar system.

atmosphere A shell of gases kept around a planet, star, or other object by its gravity.

comet A chunk of rock and ice from the edge of the solar system. Close to the Sun, its melting ices form a coma and a tail.

constellation A star pattern in the sky and the area around it.

galaxy A large system of stars, gas, and dust with anything from millions to trillions of stars.

gravity A natural force created around objects with mass, which draws other objects toward them.

light-year The distance light travels in a year—about 5.9 trillion miles (9.5 quadrillion km).

lunar eclipse When the full Moon passes into Earth's shadow so direct sunlight does not reach its surface.

Milky Way Our home galaxy, a spiral with a bar across its core. Our solar system is about 28,000 light-years from the monster black hole at its heart.

Moon Earth's closest companion in space, a ball of rock that orbits Earth every 27.3 days. Most other planets in the solar system have moons of their own.

nebula A cloud of gas or dust floating in space. Nebulae are the raw material used to make stars.

orbit A fixed path taken by one object in space around another because of the effect of gravity.

planet A world that orbits the Sun, which has enough mass and gravity to pull itself into a balllike shape, and clear space around it of other large objects.

pole star A star that lies close to Earth's north or south pole, and so stays more or less fixed in the sky as Earth rotates.

red dwarf A small, faint star with a cool red surface and less than half the mass of the Sun.

satellite Any object orbiting a planet. Moons are natural satellites made of rock and ice. Artificial (manmade) satellites are machines in orbit around Earth.

solar eclipse When the Moon passes directly in front of the Sun, casting its shadow onto Earth.

space probe A robot vehicle that explores the solar system and sends back signals to Earth.

telescope A device that collects light or other radiations from space and uses them to create a bright, clear image. Telescopes can use either a lens or a mirror to collect light.

zodiac Twelve constellations surrounding the Sun's yearly path around Earth's sky. The planets and Moon are usually found within these constellations.

Further Information

BOOKS

Daynes, Katie. *See Inside Space*. London, UK: Usborne Publishing, 2008.

DK Reference. *Space!* New York, NY: DK Publishing, 2015.

Murphy, Glenn. *Space: The Whole Whizz-Bang Story* (Science Sorted). New York, NY: Macmillan Children's Books, 2013.

Newman, Ben. *Professor Astro Cat's Frontiers of Space*. London, UK: Flying Eye Books, 2013.

Rogers, Simon. *Information Graphics: Space*. Somerville, MA: Big Picture Press, 2015.

Smithsonian. *Eyewitness Explorer: Night Sky Detective*. New York, NY: DK Publishing, 2015.

WEBSITES

www.nasa.gov/kidsclub/index.html
Join Nebula at NASA Kids' Club to play games and learn about space.

www.ngkids.co.uk/science-and-nature/ten-facts-about-space
Get started with these ten great facts about space, then explore the rest of the National Geographic Kids site for more fun.

www.esa.int/esaKIDSen/
Explore this site from the European Space Agency. There's information, games, and news.

Index

A
Andromeda galaxy 7
asteroids 4
atmosphere 8, 12, 14, 18, 26
aurorae 18–19, 27, 29
autumn 10, 11
axis 10

B
binoculars 6, 7

C
climate 10
comets 4, 14, 20–21
   67P 21
   Hale-Bopp 21
   Halley 27
   Tempel 1 21
constellations 22, 23, 24, 25, 29
corona 12
cosmic dust 4, 14, 26

D
de Lacaille, Nicolas-Louis 24
Deep Impact (space probe) 21

E
Earth 7, 8, 10, 12, 13, 14, 16,
   18, 22, 26, 28
eclipses 12–13, 26, 28
equator 19, 22, 24

F
fireball 14

G
galaxies 4, 22
gravity 5
Greenwich Meridian 8

H
Hipparchus 26
horizon 9, 23, 25

I
International Date Line 8

J
Jupiter 20

L
Leonid meteor shower 14, 15

M
meteor 14, 15, 29
Meteor Crater 16, 17
meteorites 16
Milky Way 5, 22
Moctezuma II 20
Moon 6, 9, 12, 13, 16, 18,
   19, 26, 28

N
nebulae 4
noctilucent clouds 19
north pole 9

P
planets 4, 14, 18, 28
Polaris 10, 22, 27
precession 10
Ptolemy 22

R
Rosetta (space probe) 21

S
seasons 10, 11
sky 8
solar system 18, 20
solar wind 18, 19, 20
south pole 9
spring 10, 11
summer 10, 11
Sun 4, 8, 10, 11, 12, 13, 14,
   18, 19, 20, 26
superclusters 4, 5
supergiants 4

T
telescopes 6
time zones 8

U
UFOs 14

W
winter 10, 11

Z
zodiacal light 18

DEPRESSION &
MENTAL HEALTH

PETE SANDERS and STEVE MYERS

COPPER BEECH BOOKS
BROOKFIELD, CONNECTICUT

An Aladdin Book
© Aladdin Books Ltd 1996
© U.S. text 1998
All rights reserved

Designed and produced by
Aladdin Books Ltd
28 Percy Street
London W1P 0LD

First published
in the United States in 1998 by
Copper Beech Books,
an imprint of
The Millbrook Press
2 Old New Milford Road
Brookfield, Connecticut 06804

Printed in Belgium

Design   David West
                Children's Books
Designer   Robert Perry
Editor   Alex Edmonds
Picture research Brooks Krikler
                Research
Illustrator   Mike Lacey

**Library of Congress
Cataloging-in-Publication Data**
Sanders, Pete.
Depression and mental health / Pete Sanders
and Steve Myers ; illustrated by Mike Lacey.
p. cm. — (What do you know about)
Includes index.
Summary: Discusses depression and other
aspects of mental health, and the effects such
illnesses can have on the depressed person and
those around him.
ISBN 0-7613-0802-4 (lib. bdg.)
1. Depression, Mental—Juvenile literature.
2. Depression in children—Juvenile literature.
3. Mental health—Juvenile literature.
[1. Depression, Mental. 2. Mental health.]
I. Myers, Steve. II. Lacey, Mike, ill.
III. Title. IV. Series: Sanders, Pete.
What do you know about.
RC537.S364 1998   97-41647
616.85'27—dc21   CIP AC

5 4 3 2 1

CONTENTS

HOW TO USE THIS BOOK............................2

INTRODUCTION 3

EMOTIONAL HEALTH 4

WHAT IS DEPRESSION?...........................7

CAUSES OF DEPRESSION.........................11

OTHER MENTAL HEALTH PROBLEMS 14

EFFECTS ON PEOPLE'S LIVES 18

STRESS AND MENTAL HEALTH 21

WHAT HELP IS AVAILABLE?....................24

LOOKING AFTER YOURSELF 27

WHAT CAN WE DO?..............................30

INDEX 32

HOW TO USE THIS BOOK
The books in this series are intended to help young people to understand more about issues that may affect their lives.

Each book can be read by a child alone, or together with a parent, teacher, or guardian. Issues raised in the storyline are further discussed in the accompanying text, so that there is an opportunity to talk through ideas as they come up.

At the end of the book there is a section called "What Can We Do?" This gives practical ideas that will be useful for both young people and adults. Organizations and helplines are also listed, to provide the reader with additional sources of information and support.